2017

To Claire,
celebrating
your deep love +
joy for
Alex
and
Hazel

With love,
Mary Ann

JIGGY JOG PRESS

To My Child

ISBN # 978-0-692-81137-5

Written by Jennifer Johnston Schroeder
Hand lettered and illustrated by Laura Hutton McCranner
Graphic Layout by Sarah Wolters

Published by Jiggy Jog Press, Holland, MI, 49423
www.jiggyjogpress.com

Holland Litho Printing Service, Holland, Michigan www.hollandlitho.com

With love and gratitude, I dedicate this book to my beautiful daughters, Hannah and Kailey.

You are my inspiration.

You were born into eager arms;
cradled in love;
wrapped with promise...

...and joy swelled within my heart
beyond anything I could have ever imagined.

You were born and I knew my mother
and all of my grandmothers before her
had given me the movement and capacity
to nurture you.

We rocked together for hours.

We rocked.
Angels convened around us.

I sang to you...

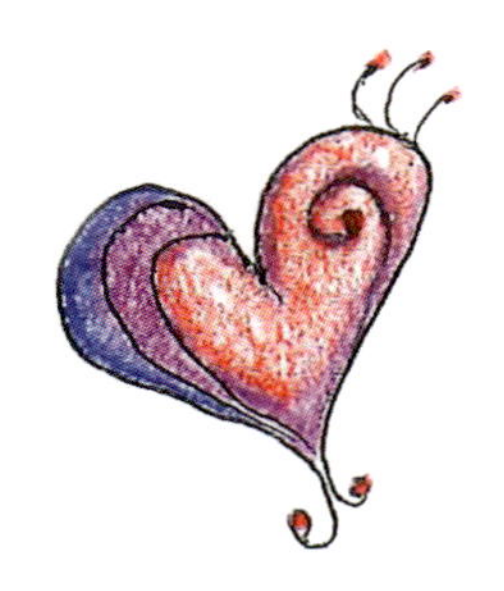

...whispering to your tiny ears.

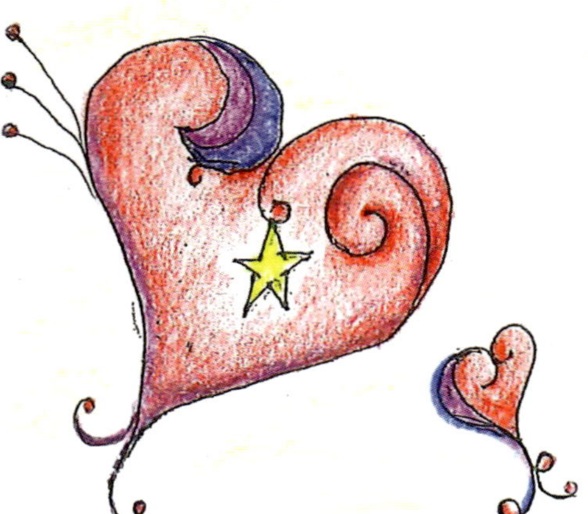

I stroked your head.

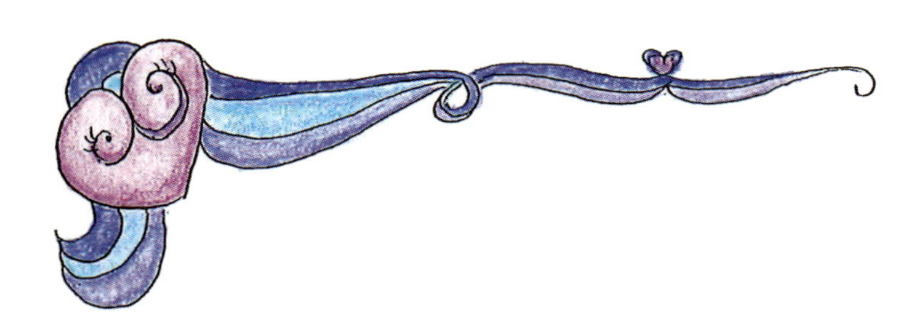

I was mesmerized

by your infant fingers and toes.

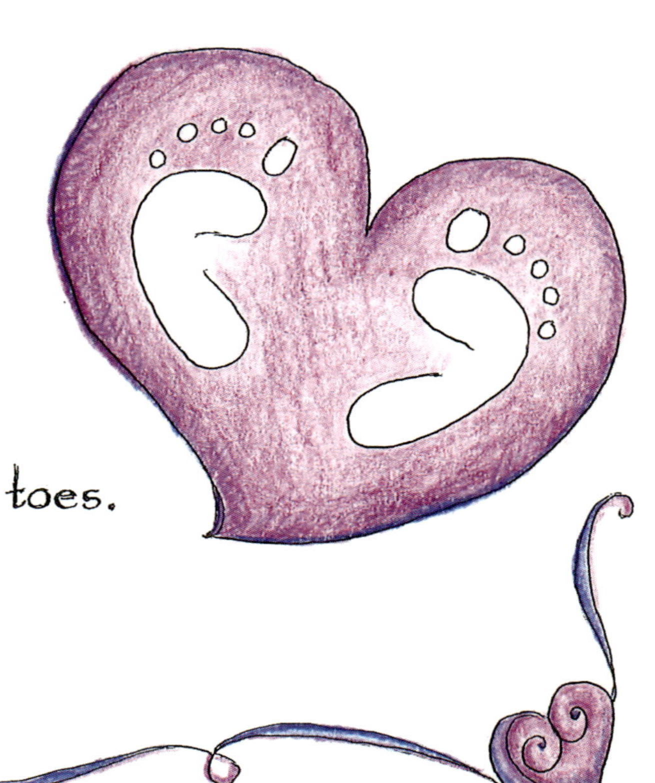

You were born and I had never
seen anything more beautiful or perfect.

I loved your baby lips.

I kissed your cheeks thousands of times.

You were born and our ancestors gathered once again to celebrate the continuity of life.

Generations co-mingled and refined to bring
forth hope, once again.

You were born into the inheritance
and expectation of goodness and value...

...grace, gifted through Love.

You were born into the vision for the future...

...to carry this Love along.

You were born into eager arms;

cradled in love;

wrapped in possibilities.

You were born
and at that moment I knew...

I will always love you.

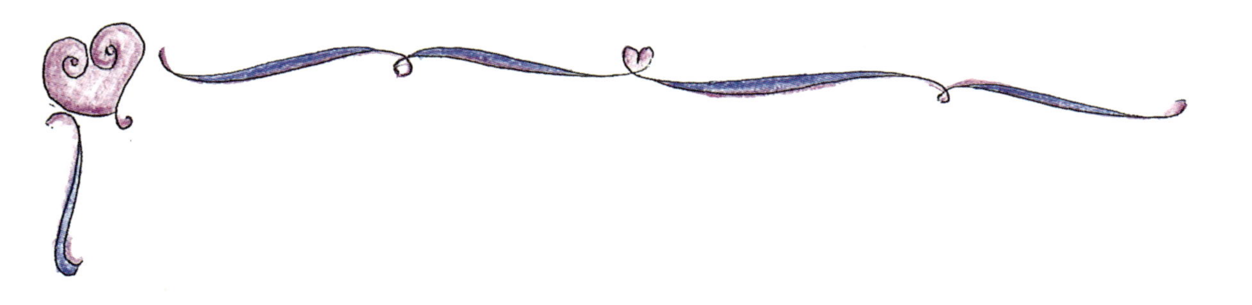

Thank you to MaryMartha Melendy for proofing the punctuation.

A huge thank you to Laura Hutton McCranner for bringing text to life with her magical artwork.

Thank you to Sarah Wolters who pulled it all together with an artistic eye and diligent technical skills.

Kailey, Jennifer, Hannah
ca. 1992

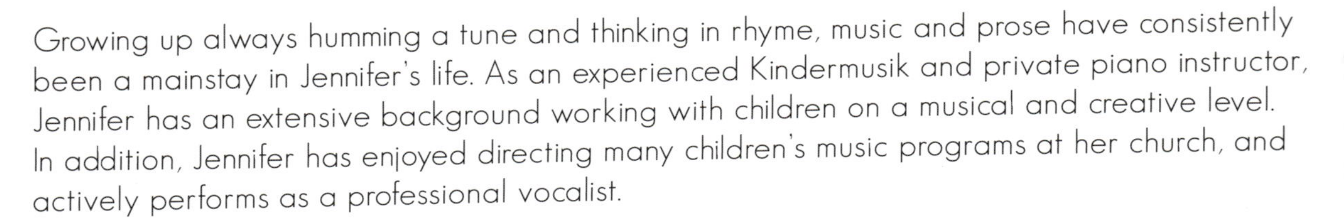

Growing up always humming a tune and thinking in rhyme, music and prose have consistently been a mainstay in Jennifer's life. As an experienced Kindermusik and private piano instructor, Jennifer has an extensive background working with children on a musical and creative level. In addition, Jennifer has enjoyed directing many children's music programs at her church, and actively performs as a professional vocalist.

A love and commitment to music and poetry has always been, and will continue to be, woven into the fabric of Jennifer's life. This love is also shared by her husband Karl and their two daughters, Hannah and Kailey, who are also professional musicians.

Photo credit:
Melissa Winchester

Laura Hutton McCranner has been involved in art from a very young age, attending art classes at the university of Illinois throughout grade school. She is an NCIDQ certified interior designer with a degree from the University of Wisconsin-Madison. She has been practicing design for over twenty years and has had several of her projects featured on Houzz.com.

Laura and her husband, Bryan, reside in Holland, MI with their two "Coton" pups and enjoy occasional visits from their two grown children, Scott and Molly. They both tend to be workaholics but when not working they enjoy competitive yacht racing in amateur sailing events in the great lakes region.